GW00994505

Traditional Devon Recipes

Carolyn Martin

Bossiney Books

First published 2013 by Bossiney Books Ltd
33 Queens Drive, Ilkley, LS29 9QW
© 2013 Carolyn Martin
ISBN 978-1-906474-37-9
Printed in Great Britain by R Booth Ltd, Penryn, Cornwall

Contents

Author's acknowledgements

Thanks are due to the helpful staff at the Devon Record Office and the West Country
Studies Library as well as to local museums and Tourist Information Offices around
the county. I have received considerable help from the staff at National Trust
properties, notably Lydford Gorge, Arlington Court, Castle Drogo, A la Ronde and
Knightshayes Court. I would also like to thank the members of the Devon History
Society and Dr Sadru Bhanji and Paul Cleave from the Devon and Exeter Institution
for their helpful suggestions.

Introduction

At first glance, the image presented by Devon is a rural paradise – rolling green fields with grazing cows, and interspersed with clusters of caramel-licked thatched cottages nestling discreetly in the hollows.

In fact Devon is one of our largest counties and has a variety of differing landscapes, from the rocky coasts of the north, with their steep, dark cliffs, to the more exotic climes of the south, including the so-called 'English Riviera'. The harsh uplands of Dartmoor stand in between.

These varied climates and vegetation have historically provided fish from the coastal waters, beef and venison from the moorlands, and milk, fruit and vegetables from the warmer soils. It is no wonder that Devon is renowned both for the quality of its produce and the range of its cooking. Its hospitality, too, is legendary.

It also has an abundance of festivals, as fairs and traditions are revived or recreated to promote food from the county, generating income and interest – we have the traditional Goosey Fair at Tavistock and the Cheese and Onion Fayre in Newton Abbot, as well as newer events such as the Exeter Food Fair and the Plymouth Food Fest.

The recipes in this book are all taken from Devon's past but they have been adapted to suit modern tastes. They make use of traditional foods, are simple to prepare and reflect the current interest in sustainably sourced produce. From apples and plums to crabs and mackerel, there is much to choose from and to enjoy.

The cream tea deserves a special mention, as this has evolved and changed over the years. Originally a small snack provided for farm workers by the farmer's wife, nowadays it is an essential part of the holiday experience, as visitors treat themselves with a real Devon cream tea in the interval between lunch and dinner. It's a luxury not normally indulged in at home!

A note on the recipes

Both metric and imperial measurements are given for the recipes, which are generally for four people. Oven temperatures and timings are for a conventional oven: with fan ovens the cooking time can be reduced. All the recipes have been tried and tested and sampled with approval by my husband, my most discerning critic.

Soups and Starters

Chestnut soup

Apart from chestnut stuffing to accompany the roast turkey or goose at Christmas time, comparatively little use is made of chestnuts in this country. This is a shame because chestnuts are particularly nutritious, with less oil than most other nuts and containing the same proportions of protein, starch and fat as wheat products. The following recipe is adapted from a North Devon estate recipe collection, dated 1876.

Ingredients

450g (1lb) fresh chestnuts *or* 225g (8oz) ready cooked chestnuts *or* 1 tin of chestnut purée

25g (1oz) butter

2 onions, peeled and chopped

2 medium potatoes, peeled and chopped

2 sticks of celery, sliced

850ml (1 1/2 pints) chicken stock

1/4 tsp ground nutmeg

Salt and pepper

150ml (1/4 pint) fresh single cream

Fresh or dried thyme

Method

If using fresh chestnuts, cut a cross on the base of each chestnut, drop into a pan of boiling water and allow to cook for about a minute. Drain and cool, then peel off the outer skins.

Melt the butter in a large pan and add the onions, potatoes and celery, coating well with the butter before adding the peeled chestnuts. If using cooked chestnut purée, this is added at a later stage. Pour in the stock, with the ground nutmeg and salt and pepper to taste. Allow to simmer gently for about 30 minutes, until the potatoes are cooked and the chestnuts soft.

The chestnut purée is added for the last five minutes, to warm through. Liquidise the soup, re-heat and add the cream. Pour into warm soup bowls, with a scattering of fresh or dried thyme, and serve with warm croûtons.

Green pea soup

An early 19th century recipe for a summer soup when peas used to be one of the regular crops in any country garden. Nowadays, frozen or tinned peas are the norm, as peas in their shells are difficult to obtain. The original recipe suggests using '3 pints of old green peas' for the stock and young peas to finish. Here, the recipe has been adapted to use fresh or frozen peas.

Ingredients

50g (2oz) butter

1 cucumber, peeled and sliced

1 onion, sliced

1 lettuce, shredded, with any tough stalks removed

350g (12oz) fresh or frozen peas

25g (1oz) flour

700ml (1 1/4 pints) ham or strong vegetable stock

1 tsp sugar

Salt and pepper

Pinch of cayenne pepper

2 tbsp fresh single cream

Sprigs of fresh mint to garnish

Method

Melt the butter over a low heat and add the sliced cucumber, onion and finely shredded lettuce and soften in the butter for about 10 minutes. Stir in the flour before slowly pouring in the stock. Once combined, add the sugar and seasonings with the peas, and cook again for around half an hour. Pass through a sieve or liquidise and ladle into hot soup bowls, garnishing with swirls of single cream and sprigs of fresh mint.

Devon fish soup

Sustainability and local sourcing are combined in this typical Devon fish soup, which uses some of the lesser known and less threatened species, such as ling or pollack. However a fish soup is a traditional and economical way of using up left-over fish from the market, and any firm fish fillets can be used, including smoked cod or haddock. These are added towards the end of the cooking period. The quantities and balance of fish and vegetables can be varied according to taste.

Ingredients

25 g (1 oz) butter

2 cloves of garlic, peeled and crushed

2 onions, peeled and sliced

2 carrots, peeled and sliced

2 leeks, washed and sliced

1 medium potato, peeled and chopped finely

2 sticks of celery, sliced

25 g (1 oz) plain flour

450 g (1 lb) tomatoes (chopped) *or* a large can of chopped tomatoes

850 ml (1 1/2 pints) fish stock

275 ml (1/2 pint) dry white wine

1 bay leaf

Salt and pepper to taste

700 g (1 1/2 lb) local fish fillets

150 ml (1/4 pint) Devonshire single cream

1 tbsp fresh parsley, chopped

Method

Melt the butter in a large saucepan and add the onions. Cook until softened before adding the garlic and prepared vegetables. Allow the vegetables to cook for about 3 minutes, then stir in the flour. Add the chopped tomatoes, then the fish stock and wine. Season to taste, add the bay leaves and simmer for 30 minutes, until the vegetables are cooked but not too soft. Cut the fish into bite sized cubes and add to the soup, cooking for 5-10 minutes. Pour in the single cream and serve in warm soup bowls, with a scattering of parsley.

Buttered shrimps/prawns

An early West Country recipe and a simple dish to prepare. As a modern twist, a hint of paprika can be added to give the shrimps or prawns a rosy hue. Serve with triangles of toast as a light starter or with a salad for a more substantial meal.

Ingredients

225g (8oz) peeled shrimps or prawns, fresh or frozen

150ml (1/4 pint) white wine

50g (2oz) butter

4 large free range eggs

1/4 tsp grated nutmeg

1/4 tsp paprika pepper (optional)

Salt and pepper

Few sprigs of fresh coriander

Method

Simmer the shrimps or prawns in the wine, with the nutmeg and seasonings, for about 5 minutes. Melt the butter in another saucepan and add the beaten eggs. Once the mixture thickens, add the shrimps/prawns and wine and cook gently until creamy. Do not over-cook. Spoon into serving dishes, decorate with coriander leaves and serve with triangles of brown toast, buttered or un-buttered.

Anchovy butter

Anchovies have always been caught off the south coast of Devon and with climate change and warmer seas, they are now locally more plentiful than ever.

Ingredients

225g (8oz) unsalted butter, softened

2 small (50g/2oz) tins of anchovy fillets

Black pepper and a little lemon juice

Parsley to decorate

Method

Drain the tins of anchovy fillets, patting the anchovies dry on kitchen paper. Turn into a large bowl, chop and mash well before blending with the softened butter, adding black pepper and a dash of lemon juice. When well mixed, lay the anchovy butter on a long sheet of greaseproof paper and shape into a roll. Twist in the paper and leave to harden in the fridge. To serve, slice into thin rounds and arrange on a plate, decorating with sprigs of parsley.

Anchovy butter is a useful addition to grilled fish or can be spread on savoury crackers.

Oven-baked eggs

A recipe adapted from a North Devon nineteenth century estate recipe book. The addition of herbs and cheese make these oven baked eggs not only different but quite special.

Ingredients

    4 eggs

    1 heaped tsp mixed herbs

    4 tsp grated Parmesan cheese

    4 tsp breadcrumbs, white or brown

    Salt and pepper to taste

Method

Butter the sides and bases of four small ramekins and sprinkle with mixed herbs. Break an egg into each ramekin and cover with the cheese, breadcrumbs, salt and pepper. Bake in a moderate oven, 180°C/350°F/Gas 4 for around 10 minutes, until the whites of the eggs are set.

The eggs can be served for breakfast or with spinach as a supper dish.

Edwardian potted cheese

A recipe regularly served at the National Trust property Castle Drogo. The strength of the cheese can be varied according to preference. Serve with fresh bread or savoury scones or spread generously on warm toast.

Ingredients

225 g (8 oz) Cheddar cheese, finely grated

85 g (3 oz) melted unsalted butter

1 tsp dry English mustard

1 tbsp white wine vinegar

A few drops of Tabasco sauce

Chopped walnuts

Sprigs of parsley to decorate

Method

Combine the cheese with the mustard, vinegar and Tabasco, and mix with the melted butter, beating until all the ingredients are thoroughly combined. Spoon into four small ramekins, pressing down well. Decorate with chopped walnuts and sprigs of parsley. Keep in the fridge until needed.

Visitors to Tavistock Real Cheese Fair in August might be bowled over to see the wide variety of Devon cheeses for sale, some 25-30 in all. Many have evocative names, such as Belstone (a cow's milk hard cheese), Curworthy (a creamy semi-hard cheese) or Norsworthy (a semi-hard goat's milk cheese). Exmoor Blue is the only Devon blue cheese with PGI (Protected Geographical Indication) status but there are other varieties, including Devon Blue, Harbourne Blue, from goat's milk, or Beenleigh Blue from ewe's milk.

Most of these Devon cheeses have only been produced since the 1990s but they are based on traditional recipes. During World War 2 farmhouse cheese-making went into decline, as scarce resources of milk were channelled into the factories to make Cheddar-type hard cheeses. Mass production continued in the decades after the war and the revival is a recent phenomenon.

Cheese and onion pasty

Devon pasties have a variety of fillings and are different from Cornish pasties. The following recipe for a cheese and onion pasty is from Newton Abbot.

Ingredients for the pastry (sufficient for four pasties)

450g (1lb) strong white flour

Pinch of salt

110g (4oz) hard margarine

110g (4oz) lard

200ml (7 fl oz) water

Method

Sieve the flour and salt into a large bowl and rub in the margarine and lard. Mix in sufficient water to give a soft pastry dough, knead lightly and leave to chill in the fridge.

Ingredients for one pasty (approximate)

1 small onion, chopped finely

50g (2oz) turnip, finely sliced

Salt and pepper to taste

50g (2oz) finely grated Cheddar cheese

1 medium potato, cut into thin slices

Milk and beaten egg for brushing

Method

Roll out the pastry to a 20cm (8 inch) round. Cover with the chopped onion and sliced turnip, then season with salt and pepper before sprinkling the grated cheese over the vegetables.

Top this with the sliced potato, dampen the edges of the pastry, then seal and crimp by bringing the edges of the pastry together, either at the side or across the top, pinching and twisting to form a rope-like edge.

Cut a small air vent in the pasty and brush with milk and egg before baking in a hot oven 200°C/400°F/Gas 6 for 15 minutes, reducing the temperature to 180°C/350°F/Gas 4 for a further 30-40 minutes, until golden brown.

Vegetables

Jugged celery

To 'jug' is simply to cook in an ovenproof jug or jar and usually refers to jugged hare or kipper. Jugged celery is an old Devon dish and provides an interesting and unusual accompaniment to fish, poultry or roast meats, such as venison, lamb or pork. The celery retains its shape during cooking and, when served in a large oval dish, it graces any dining table. If a softer texture is preferred, the celery can be cooked horizontally in a wide container or bain-marie.

Ingredients

450g (1lb) Bramley cooking apples, peeled, cored and quartered

2 tbsp brown sugar (or more according to taste)

2 rashers back bacon, one whole and the other chopped

1 head of celery, washed and trimmed

1 onion, chopped finely

3 whole cloves

1/4 tsp chopped fresh rosemary

Salt and pepper to taste

(Optional – a few chopped walnuts, sprinkled over the chopped bacon)

Method

Stew apples and sugar with 1 tbsp water on a low heat until soft. Place the whole rasher of bacon on the base of a strong, tall 1.2 litre or 2 pint ovenproof jug, 10-12cm (4-5 inches) in diameter, and pour in the stewed apple.

Push the celery sticks into the apple and sprinkle with the seasonings and chopped onion. Trim the tops of the celery sticks with scissors, so that they are level with the top of the jug and push the shorter cut pieces into the jug around the celery sticks.

Spread the chopped bacon over the celery and cover closely with foil, before placing the jug in a pan of boiling water, with the water coming half way up the sides. Check on the water levels from time to time and simmer for approximately 2 1/2 hours. Pour into a large oval dish to serve.

A dish of onions

An Edwardian recipe, which stands as a vegetable dish in its own right or as an accompaniment to fish.

Ingredients

3 large onions

1 small leek, sliced

275 ml (1/2 pint) milk

25 g (1 oz) butter

25 g (1 oz) plain flour

3 hard boiled eggs

Salt and pepper to taste

Method

Boil the onions in salted water until tender. Strain and spoon into a greased pie dish, with a scattering of sliced leeks. Reserve 275 ml (1/2 pint) of the onion water. Melt the butter in a small saucepan, stir in the flour and cook for a few minutes before slowly adding the liquid – the onion water and milk.

Once it's incorporated, heat slowly and cook gently for about 2 minutes. Slice the hard boiled eggs into the sauce, add the salt and pepper and pour over the onions. Bake in a moderate oven 180°C/350°F/Gas 4 for 20 minutes. Serve at once.

Green peas with lettuce

An unusual recipe found in a Devon estate collection from the 1870s.

Ingredients

Peas, lettuce and butter. The quantities depending on appetites but generally allowing a quarter of a lettuce to 'a pint of peas' (570 ml), finishing with 25 g (1 oz) butter.

Method

Boil the peas until tender and add the shredded lettuce, cooking until just wilted. Drain, add the butter and once melted, serve.

Teddie or Potato cake

A variation of the Devon pot cake or Crediton pan cake is the Devon teddie cake (teddie is a Devon word for potato) and recipes for potato cakes appear in most old Devon cookery books.

As with the pot cake, which makes use of basic ingredients available in any store cupboard, teddie cakes can be cooked in a variety of ways, sweet with sugar and currants or savoury with cheese. They are quickly made and eaten hot, straight from the oven or hob, split open and generously buttered or if sweet, sprinkled with sugar – delicious.

Ingredients

110g (4oz) cooked, mashed potato

175g (6oz) self-raising flour

85g (3oz) suet, butter or dripping

25g (1oz) granulated sugar

25-50g (1-2oz) currants

$^1/_2$ tsp ground cinnamon

Or for savoury potato cakes, replace the sugar, currants and cinnamon with a pinch of salt, $^1/_4$ tsp grated nutmeg and 25-50g (1-2oz) grated cheese.

Method

Sift the flour and cinnamon together and rub in the butter, suet or dripping, then add the mashed potatoes (once they have cooled), followed by the sugar and currants (or cheese). If too dry to handle, moisten with a little milk or stock before rolling out into a circle, about 20cm (8 inch) in diameter.

Place on a greased baking sheet and bake in a hot oven 190°C/375°F/ Gas 5 for about 30 minutes. Alternatively, the mixture can be cooked in a greased frying pan, 20-23cm (8-9 inch) in diameter, cooked slowly and browned on both sides.

Serve hot, sprinkled with sugar or spread with butter for the savoury variety.

Parsnip cakes

Parsnip cakes are made in the same way as Devon potato cake but shaped into small patties or cakes before being cooked on the hob.

Ingredients

450g (1lb) cooked parsnips, mashed with butter

2 tbsp plain flour

1 tea-cup of breadcrumbs, white or brown

1 beaten egg

25g (1oz) softened butter

Method

Mix the mashed parsnips with the flour and breadcrumbs. Bind together with the beaten egg and softened butter. Shape into small, flat cakes and cook for around 10 minutes in a greased frying pan on the hob, turning until both sides are evenly browned.

Parsnip cakes make a versatile accompaniment to a variety of dishes – try them with bacon and egg for breakfast or to accompany fish.

Parsnips and apple

Mashing together equal quantities of cooked parsnips and apples, with butter and ground nutmeg, makes an interesting vegetable dish for any occasion.

Green kidney beans

It is said that people in Crediton served their green kidney beans in a very different way, cooked whole rather than sliced. A mound of beans topped with a large lamb chop made a complete meal.

A West Country vegetable casserole

With the unusual addition of pears, this is a recipe for a cold winter's day, when the root vegetables in the garden are at their best. A real West Country recipe, using local cider and cider vinegar. The mix of vegetables can be varied and the casserole spiced up with the addition of herbs and spices, such as celery salt or chilli powder. For non-vegetarians, smoked sausage could be mixed with the layered vegetables.

Serve with a green vegetable and, if cooked in the summer months, try peas with lettuce cooked in the Devon way. (See page 13.)

Ingredients

1 onion, peeled and sliced

1/4 swede, peeled and cubed

3 parsnips, peeled and sliced

2 medium potatoes, peeled and sliced

1 leek, washed and cut into 2 cm (1 inch) slices

2 pears, cored and sliced

85 g (3 oz) Cheddar cheese, coarsely grated

3 heaped tbsp breadcrumbs, white or brown

150 ml (1/4 pint) dry Devonshire cider

1 tbsp cider vinegar

50 g (2 oz) butter

1 tbsp chopped parsley

Salt and pepper

Method

Boil the prepared vegetables for about 10 minutes, drain and then layer them in a large casserole with the uncooked pears. Season with salt and pepper before pouring over the cider and cider vinegar. Mix the cheese and breadcrumbs with the chopped parsley, scatter over the surface and dot with knobs of butter. Bake for 40-45 minutes at 190°C/375°F/Gas 5 until the vegetables are cooked and the thatched cheesy topping golden brown.

Fish

Fish pudding

This is from an 1846 recipe collection by a Victorian clergyman, from Exeter.

Ingredients

350g (12oz) local white fish, well poached

2 tbsp breadcrumbs, white or brown

1/2 tsp cayenne pepper

1/2 tbsp anchovy essence, or more according to taste

3 eggs

150ml (1/4 pint) single cream

Sprigs of parsley for decoration

Method

Flake the poached fish and mix with the breadcrumbs, cayenne pepper and anchovy essence. Beat the eggs with the cream and add to the fish mixture. Spoon this into a well-greased 600ml or 1 pint pudding basin, and steam for an hour. Turn out of the basin to serve, decorating with a few sprigs of parsley.

Note – the pudding can be varied by adding a little cooked smoked haddock and/or chopped leeks before cooking, to give more colour.

Brixham is the main fishing port along the South Devon coast, where fish is brought in daily for the markets. The wide variety of local fresh fish include sea bass, turbot, pollack, ling, cod, haddock, plaice and both lemon and Dover sole.

Herring are more plentiful along the North Devon coast: in Clovelly they are called 'silver darlings' and honoured with an annual herring festival.

Veesh pie or Haddock in scrumpy

Veesh is a Devon dialect pronunciation of fish. The combination of fish, cider and cheese gives the pie an unusual but surprisingly tasty flavour.

Ingredients

450g (1lb) haddock or cod fillet

8 mushrooms, sliced

2 large tomatoes, sliced

275ml (1/2 pint) Devon cider

25g (1oz) butter

25g (1oz) plain flour

50g (2oz) Cheddar cheese, grated

Salt and pepper to taste

Method

Cut the fish into bite-sized pieces and arrange in a greased ovenproof casserole. Layer with sliced mushrooms and tomatoes, then cover with the cider, adding salt and pepper to taste. Bake at 180°C/350°F/Gas 4 for 20 minutes.

Remove the casserole from the oven. Pour off and reserve the cooked cider. Melt the butter in a small pan and mix in the flour before adding the cider, making up to 275ml (1/2 pint) with water or vegetable stock.

Cook on a medium heat for three minutes, stirring frequently, before adding to the cooked fish and vegetables. Cover with grated cheese and return to the oven for 10-15 minutes to brown the cheese. This can also be done under a heated grill.

Serve with mashed potatoes and a green vegetable, such as curly kale.

Trout in newspaper with gooseberry sauce

Cooking fish *'en papillote'* (or in paper) was a popular way of baking fish at the beginning of the twentieth century. In 1911-12 there were no less than five books published on the subject. In Devon the traditional way was to cook fish in dampened newspaper. Nowadays cooking in greaseproof paper is preferred.

Ingredients

1 trout per person

3 sheets of greaseproof paper per fish

A selection of fresh herbs, according to season (parsley, marjoram, thyme, sage)

Zest of 1 medium lemon

Large knob of butter per fish

Method

Gut each trout, without removing any bones and wash well. Fill the body with the herbs, lemon zest and butter. Wrap each fish in three sheets of greaseproof paper and thoroughly dampen in running water. Place on a baking sheet and cook in a hot oven, 200°C/400°F/Gas 6 for 15-20 minutes. Remove the paper with scissors, to reveal the pink and succulent flesh of the trout. The skin will come away with the paper and the exposed bones can be removed quite easily.

Serve with gooseberry sauce or a sharp yogurt sauce, with mint, chives and lemon juice. Jugged celery would also go well with the trout.

Ingredients for the gooseberry sauce

225g (8oz) gooseberries

150ml (1/4 pint) dry cider

2 tbsp granulated sugar

1/4 tsp mace or nutmeg

25g (1oz) butter

Method

Add the sugar and nutmeg to the gooseberries and cook in the cider until soft. Sieve or liquidise the sauce and reheat, adding the butter before serving with the trout.

Kedgeree

Kedgeree originates from India, where the dish usually contains rice, lentils, limes and spices, as well as smoked fish. The following recipe is adapted from an 1846 recipe collection, held at the National Trust property, Arlington Court.

Ingredients

225 g (8 oz) boiled long grain rice

350 g (12 oz) cooked white fish, such as haddock, pollack or ling

110 g (4 oz) smoked mackerel, with a small quantity of dried fish, if available

3 hard boiled eggs

2 tbsp chopped parsley plus extra for garnishing

1-2 chillies, chopped

2 anchovies, chopped

1/2 tsp mixed dried herbs

Salt and pepper to taste

1 dsp chutney, or to taste, choosing a variety that is not too sweet

25 g (1 oz) butter

Method

Flake the white fish and smoked mackerel into the boiled rice, then add the chopped chillies, anchovies, salt to taste, and herbs. The dried fish is an optional addition. Slice and chop the hard boiled eggs and add these, with the chutney. Dot with butter and cook in moderate oven 180°C/350°F/Gas 4 for approximately 30 minutes, garnishing with the extra parsley before serving.

Bread and butter pudding with crab and mushrooms

Many traditional dishes from Devon make use of left-over bread, usually sweet, as with bread and butter pudding which has eggs, currants and cream. The following nineteenth century recipe is unusual, being a savoury version with crab, which is particularly plentiful along the South Devon coast.

Ingredients

6 slices of white bread, buttered and with the crusts removed

110g (4oz) crabmeat, brown and white, fresh or tinned

Salt, pepper and 1/4 tsp cayenne pepper

1 small onion, finely chopped

25g (1oz) butter

110g (4oz) sliced mushrooms, different varieties if possible

1 tbsp fresh parsley, chopped

1 tbsp Parmesan cheese (grated)

110ml (4 fl oz) milk

110ml (4 fl oz) single cream

2 free range eggs

50g (2oz) strong Cheddar cheese, grated

1 small leek, chopped finely

Method

Melt the butter in a small saucepan, add the chopped onion and cook until softened. Add the mushrooms and cook for a few minutes to remove some of the liquid.

Leave to cool before adding the parsley and the Parmesan cheese. Meanwhile, add salt, pepper and cayenne to the crab, then using the buttered slices of bread, make sandwiches of the mushroom mixture and the seasoned crab. Place these in a large buttered ovenproof dish.

Beat the eggs into the milk and cream, season to taste and pour over the sandwiches. Leave to soak in for about 2 hours. Push the sliced leeks into the liquid and grate the Cheddar cheese over the pudding before baking in a moderately hot oven 190°C/375°F/Gas 5 for 30-40 minutes, until the top is crisp and brown and the custard is set. Serve at once, with a green or tomato salad.

Meat

Dartmouth pie

Originally, Dartmouth pie was made with layers of meat (mutton or pork), suet and dried fruit, sprinkled with sugar and nutmeg, then covered with a pastry topping. The resulting dish was supposed to keep well during sea journeys and fortify the sailors as they left Dartmouth for far-away places. The following recipe is still made in some Dartmouth restaurants today.

Ingredients

225 g (8 oz) shortcrust pastry

4 pork (or lamb) chops, boned and de-fatted

2 onions, peeled and sliced

4 medium cooking apples, peeled, cored and sliced

1/2 tsp grated nutmeg

1 tbsp granulated sugar

25 g (1 oz) currants (optional)

275 ml (1/2 pint) dry cider

Method

Place the chops in a large ovenproof casserole and cover with alternate layers of apples and onions, nutmeg and sugar, sprinkling the layers with the currants. Add the cider before covering with a shortcrust pastry topping. Brush with milk and make slashes in the pastry for the steam to escape.

Bake at 200°C/400°F/Gas 6 for 20 minutes, then lower the oven temperature to 150°C/300°F/Gas 2 for about an hour. Cover with foil towards the end of the cooking time to prevent browning.

Dartmouth Pie can be served with Devonshire cream, single, double or clotted.

Crocky pie

Crocky pie or hot pot is cooked in many different ways. In Lancashire the stew – generally of lamb or mutton – is cooked under a topping of sliced potatoes, which are browned to a dark crispness in the oven. In Somerset crocky pie has an oven-baked suet crust, whereas in Devon crocky pie is steamed, with the potatoes layered over the suet crust.

Ingredients for the suet crust

110g (4oz) self-raising flour

50g (2oz) suet

Pinch of salt

6 tbsp cold water

For the pie

Chopped vegetables, depending on the season – carrots, onion, parsnips, turnips, celery – the quantity depending on the size of the basin

Slices of cold cooked meat, preferably lamb

1 Bramley cooking apple, peeled, cored and sliced

Fresh mixed herbs (parsley, sage, thyme, marjoram) and seasoning

Topping

4 medium sized potatoes, preferably new, washed and scrubbed

Method

Fill a 1.2 litre or 2 pint basin three-quarters full with layers of pre-pared chopped vegetables, apple and meat, sprinkling with the herbs and seasoning. Add a cupful of good lamb stock. Mix the flour and suet with the water and roll out sufficient suet pastry to fit on to the top of the basin – a pan lid makes a good cutter – pushing down over the vegetables. Cut the potatoes into thin slices and lay over the suet topping. Cover with foil, securing well, then place the basin over a pan of water. Steam for 2-3 hours, checking that there is a good level of water in the pan.

To serve

Remove the potatoes from the top and cut the suet crust into por-tions. Spoon out the vegetables and meat, and serve with a slice of crust and a few potatoes on each plate.

Rabbit pudding

Rabbits formed a valuable part of the daily diet in the past and they are widely available today, either farmed or wild. This recipe for rabbit pudding, complete with the suet topping, has been adapted for the slow cooker although it can be cooked equally successfully by covering the suet topping closely with foil and cooking on a low setting (140°C/275°F/Gas 1) in a conventional oven.

Ingredients

700g (1 1/2 lb) rabbit, cut into jointed serving pieces

25g (1oz) butter

1 onion

1 tbsp flour

570ml (1 pint) chicken stock

2 tomatoes, chopped

1 tbsp tomato purée

1 tsp mixed herbs, salt and pepper to taste

Method

Dry the joints of rabbit with kitchen paper. Heat the butter in a large frying pan and fry the rabbit until golden in colour, then transfer to the pre-heated slow cooker. Fry the onion in the remaining fat, until transparent, before stirring in the flour and gradually incorporating the stock. Bring to the boil and add the tomatoes, the purée, herbs and seasonings. Pour over the rabbit.

Ingredients for the suet crust

175g (6oz) self-raising flour   pinch of salt

85g (3oz) suet   cold water to mix

Method

Mix the dry ingredients and add sufficient cold water to make a pliable dough, as a soft pastry. Roll the pastry to the size of the slow cooker lid, moisten the edges with cold water and place over the rabbit, pressing the edges into the pot.

Once the rabbit casserole reaches boiling point, cook on a low setting for at least 5 hours, until the rabbit is tender. Slice the suet crust into serving portions and remove the larger rabbit bones before serving.

Roast goose

Ingredients

4.5kg (10lb) goose

570ml (1 pint) dry cider

Salt and pepper

Method

There are many ways of preparing goose, but to obtain a crisp finish, pierce the skin with a sharp knife and pour boiling water over the bird. Allow to dry before roasting. Rub salt and pepper over the body and fill with a chosen stuffing. There is no need to add extra fat to the goose before cooking but 570ml (1 pint) of cider can be added to the roasting tin and the goose basted with the liquid from time to time. Roast at 220°C/425°F/Gas 7 for 30 minutes, then reduce the temperature to 180°C/350°F/Gas 4 for about 2 1/2 hours. Leave to rest for 30 minutes before carving.

An added bonus is all the delicious goose fat or dripping collected during cooking. In the past dripping was much used in the kitchen and visitors used to go to one Exeter hotel specially to sample the dripping cake, but sadly no longer. (See page 42.)

Traditional stuffings for roast goose were either a sage and onion stuffing or the following:

Ingredients for apple and rum stuffing

4 eating apples, sliced

150ml (1/4 pint) dark rum

110g (4oz) fresh breadcrumbs, white or brown

1 chopped onion

A few leaves of fresh sage

1/2 tsp ground nutmeg

Goose liver, sliced

Salt and pepper

Method

Soak the eating apples in the dark rum, overnight. The next day, add the breadcrumbs and other ingredients, mix well and use to stuff the bird, or cook separately.

Baked Indian curry

Surprisingly, curries feature prominently in old Devon cookery collections, possibly because the south Devon coast was a favourite location for retired Indian Army officers. By today's standards, many of the curries are bland and mild, using curry powder rather than an assortment of spices, although some Devon recipes add coconut milk as the final touch.

The following recipe, a baked curry, is rather different.

Ingredients

  1 lemon

  225g (8oz) cold, cooked meat, such as the left-overs from the roast goose

  Large teacupful of breadcrumbs, white or brown

  1 dsp curry powder

  110g (4oz) ground almonds

  1 egg

  Milk to mix

  Butter, large knob

Method

Rub a pie dish with a slice of lemon and then with butter. Mince the cooked meat or chop finely in a food processor before adding the breadcrumbs then the curry powder dissolved in a little milk. Mix well before adding the ground almonds, beating to the consistency of cake mixture with a little more milk.

Finally, add the beaten egg. Turn into the pie dish and bake in a medium oven 180°C/350°F/Gas 4 for 30 minutes. Serve in the dish with boiled rice to accompany.

The recipe suggests that a large lump of butter put on top of the baked curry as it comes out of the oven will enhance the flavour. A selection of chutneys and pickles should be made available.

Devonshire plait

Keeping a domestic pig was part of cottage living in the past and this recipe calls for one of the cheaper cuts of pork, belly pork. Minced and combined with onions and cheese, with a selection of different herbs, the plaited pastry turns a humble dish into something special.

Ingredients

340g (12oz) belly pork, minced

1 eating apple, cored and chopped

85g (3oz) mature Cheddar cheese, grated

1 medium onion, peeled and chopped

1 clove garlic, peeled and crushed

1 tbsp fine brown breadcrumbs

2 tbsp chopped parsley

Small bunch of sage leaves, together with a selection of other garden herbs to hand

Salt and pepper to taste

1 egg beaten

340g (12oz) puff pastry

Method

Cut off the rind and any unwanted fat from the pork and mince the lean meat (or chop in the food processor), then add the chopped onion, garlic, grated cheese, chopped apple, breadcrumbs, parsley, other herbs and most of the beaten egg. Season to taste.

Roll out the puff pastry into a 25cm (10 inch) square and spread the pork mixture into a roll along the centre of the pastry. To create the plaited effect, cut the pastry on each side into diagonal strips, dampen the ends and fold the strips alternately across the meat. Seal the ends and brush the whole with the remains of the beaten egg.

Transfer the roll to a greased and dampened baking tray and bake at 220°C/425°F/Gas 7 for 20 minutes, reducing the heat to 180°C/350°F/Gas 4 for a further 20-25 minutes and covering with foil towards the end of the cooking time, to prevent over browning.

Serve hot with vegetables or cold with salad.

Exeter stew with Devon suety

Exeter stew is a plain but hearty beef stew, which is often accompanied by doughboys (the Devon term for dumplings). Here the stew is served with Devon suety, an oven baked savoury suet roll.

Ingredients

900g (2lb) braising steak, cut into bite-sized pieces

2 large onions, peeled and sliced

1/2 small turnip, peeled and diced

1/2 small swede, peeled and diced

2 carrots, peeled and sliced

50g (2oz) plain flour

50g (2oz) dripping, lard or cooking oil

1.2 litres (2 pints) beef stock

1 tsp malt vinegar   Salt and pepper

Method

Remove any fat from the beef and toss the meat in a little seasoned flour. Melt the dripping in a large pan and add the meat, then fry until brown. Add the vegetables and cook gently until the onions begin to soften. Stir in the remaining seasoned flour, cooking for a few minutes before adding the beef stock and vinegar. Simmer well for about two hours, until the meat is tender. Serve with mashed potatoes, peas or green beans, together with Devon suety.

Ingredients for Devon suety

225g (8oz) plain flour   1 tsp baking powder

85g (3oz) shredded beef suet

1 onion, peeled and finely chopped

1 tsp mixed herbs   Salt and pepper

Water to mix – approximately 150ml (1/4 pint)

Method

Sieve the flour and baking powder together and then mix in the shredded suet with the chopped onion and herbs, adding salt and pepper. Mix to a soft dough with the water and roll into a sausage shape. Brush with milk and bake on a greased tray for 20 minutes in a hot oven at 200°C/400°F/Gas 6.

Puddings

Exeter pudding

The Exeter Pudding described by Mrs Beeton is 'very rich', with 7 eggs, sago and 1/4 pint of rum. Here is a more modest version, but even so it is a substantial pudding to keep out the winter cold.

Ingredients

   145g (5oz) breadcrumbs, white or brown

   85g (3oz) granulated sugar

   85g (3oz) suet

   Grated rind of 1 lemon

   6 ratafia or amaretti biscuits – optional

   3 eggs

   150ml (1/4 pint) double cream

   3 tbsp rum

   4 small sponge cakes, covered thickly with blackcurrant jam or similar

   1 tbsp breadcrumbs (white or brown) for coating

Method

Grease a round ovenproof dish well and coat the sides with the breadcrumbs. Place ratafia or amaretti biscuits on the base. Beat the eggs and sugar together and then add the rest of the breadcrumbs, suet, lemon rind, cream and rum, mixing well until all the ingredients are incorporated.

Spoon alternate layers of the cream and egg mixture with thin slices of sponge cake, generously coated with blackcurrant jam, finishing with a layer of the cream mixture. Bake at 180°C/350°F/Gas 4 for about an hour until firm, well risen and golden.

Turn out of the mould and serve with a sauce made from a few tablespoons of warm bramble jelly mixed with a little sherry.

Note The ratafia biscuits may be omitted but they do give a more attractive appearance when the pudding is served.

Apple in and out

Apple in and out can be served as a cake or pudding and the quantity of apples can be varied. Crisp outside and soft inside, with the apples sticking in and out, this is a unique dish from Devon.

Ingredients

225g (8oz) self-raising flour

110g (4oz) suet

110g (4oz) granulated sugar

2 large Bramley cooking apples, or more – up to 450g (1 1b) according to availability and taste

Milk to mix

Method

Peel, core and cut the apples into thick chunks. Mix the dry ingredients together and stir in the prepared apples. Mix with sufficient milk to give a soft consistency, without making it too wet. Turn the mixture into a greased round, large, ovenproof dish and bake at 180°C/350°F/ Gas 4 for 40-45 minutes, until golden brown.

Check the dish after half an hour and, if it is browning too quickly, cover with foil or greaseproof for the remainder of the cooking time. Serve with custard or ice cream.

Cider syllabub

Syllabubs have been popular since Elizabethan times and originally a syllabub was more of a drink, with a topping of creamy foam. Now it is a dessert of whipped cream, with wine or in this case cider.

Ingredients

1 orange

150ml (¹/₄ pint) sweet Devonshire cider

4 tbsp caster sugar

275ml (¹/₂ pint) double Devonshire cream

Method

Peel a little rind from the orange and cut into fine strips, cover with boiling water for a few minutes, then drain, refresh with cold water and reserve the rind. Meanwhile grate the remaining peel and squeeze the orange. Add the sugar to the cider, orange juice and grated peel and leave to stand for at least 2 hours.

Whip the cream until it holds its peaks, then slowly add the cider and orange liquid. Pour into serving glasses and decorate with the fine strips of orange rind. Chill for an hour before serving.

Paradise pudding

Mrs Beeton has a recipe for Paradise pudding, with brandy, in her 1859 *Book of Household Management*, but the following recipe comes from a Devon collection of recipes dated 1910. As the name suggests, it is a light and airy pudding, without any fat.

Ingredients

225g (8oz) grated cooking apples, such as Bramleys

110g (4oz) breadcrumbs, white or brown

85g (3oz) granulated sugar

3 eggs, well-beaten

Juice of an orange, with added water

Grated rind from one lemon

Salt to taste

$^1/_2$ tsp grated nutmeg

Cold water

Method

In a large basin, mix together the breadcrumbs, grated apple and sugar. Add the lemon rind, salt and nutmeg, then pour the juice of a squeezed orange into a tea cup (200ml/7 fl oz) and add water to fill to the top and add this and the beaten eggs to the mixture. Mix and beat well and turn into a greased basin, covering with foil or strong greaseproof. Steam for two hours and serve with a sweet sauce.

Paignton pudding

Paignton residents are sometimes called 'pudden eaters' and the huge Paignton pudding has had a long and sometimes turbulent history. The first of these was made in the thirteenth century to mark the granting of the town's charter. For some years it was made annually, then every fifty years or to mark a special occasion.

A pudding was made in 1859 for the opening of the railway line to Paignton but on this occasion distribution of the pudding ended in a riot, as around 18,000 residents clamoured to claim their slice.

Since then, the sizes have been smaller. A Paignton pudding was made in 2006 for the 200th anniversary of the birth of the engineer Isambard Kingdom Brunel.

The ingredients for the pudding are simple – suet, flour, raisins and eggs, with additions decided by the baker of the day. The following recipe is for a straightforward family suet pudding.

Ingredients

110g (4oz) self-raising flour

50g (2oz) breadcrumbs, white or brown

Pinch of salt

1/2 tsp ground ginger

1/4 tsp mixed spice

85g (3oz) chopped suet

110g (4oz) raisins

1 egg (beaten)

Milk to mix

Method

Mix the dry ingredients together, add the suet and raisins and mix with the beaten egg and enough milk to make a softish dough. Turn into a greased pudding basin, two-thirds filling it. Cover with grease-proof paper. Stand the basin in boiling water, cover and steam for 2 hours. Turn out and serve with golden syrup or a hot jam sauce.

Palace pudding

This is taken from a nineteenth century manuscript recipe book and is a Devon variant of Crystal Palace pudding, mentioned in Florence White's book, *Good Things in England* (1932), where the base of the mould is decorated with crystallised fruit and cherries. In the Devon version, the plain white set 'custard' contrasts well with the redcurrant jelly, creating a dish fit for a queen.

Ingredients

850 ml (1 1/2 pints) of full cream milk

20 g (3/4 oz) gelatine – vegetarian versions are available

50 g (2 oz) granulated sugar or to taste

1 tbsp orange flower water

3 large eggs

Few currants or sultanas, about 50 g (2 oz)

3-4 trifle sponges

Red currant jelly

Method

Sprinkle the gelatine into a little hot water and warm gently until dissolved, without allowing the liquid to boil. Strain the gelatine into the milk and bring to the boil. Allow to cool before adding the well-beaten eggs and cook over a gentle heat until thickened, as a custard, sweetening to taste with the sugar and flavouring with the orange flower water.

Place a few currants at the bottom of a wetted 1.2 litre or 2 pint mould and cover with the broken trifle sponges. Pour the pudding over the sponges and leave to set. Turn out and serve the pudding with generous spoonfuls of redcurrant or quince jelly.

The original recipe suggests that the pudding is best made the day before.

Devonshire junket

Junket recipes date from the seventeenth century but with the production of commercial rennet in the 1870s it became a popular Victorian nursery sweet. The secret is to add the rennet to the milk at the right temperature, not too hot or too cold. Devonshire junket is always served with Devon clotted cream.

Ingredients

570 ml (1 pint) fresh full cream milk

1 tbsp caster sugar

2 tsp rennet

1/4 tsp grated nutmeg or ground cinnamon

Devon clotted cream

Method

Warm the milk to blood heat (37°C or 98.4°F), then stir in the sugar, followed by the rennet. Pour into a deep bowl and set in a cool place for 1-2 hours, until set. Sprinkle nutmeg or cinnamon over the surface before serving with Devon clotted cream.

Treacle pudding

Traditional recipes often owe their survival to their simplicity. This treacle pudding, from an 1870 collection of Devon recipes, is one such example. Fat enriched flour is layered with spoonfuls of syrup and sugar, then baked in a moderate oven.

Ingredients

225 g (8 oz) plain flour

85 g (3 oz) fat, either dripping or butter

3 tsp baking powder

3 tbsp granulated sugar

3 tbsp golden syrup

Method

Rub the fat into the flour, before adding the baking powder. Grease a large ovenproof casserole and fill with alternate layers of flour, syrup and sugar, making sure that the top layer is of flour and the syrup is completely covered. Bake in a medium oven, 180°C/350°F/Gas 4, for 30-35 minutes.

Eat hot, straight from the oven, serving with a thick Devonshire custard and locally sourced stewed fruit, such as blackcurrants.

White pot

White pot or whitpit has long had a place in the cook's repertoire and the cookery writer Hannah Woolley (1622–c1675) includes a Devonshire White Pot in her recipe collection.

How white pot was prepared depended on where you lived. In Somerset it was a milk pudding thickened with flour, then sweetened with syrup and raisins, whereas in Devon it was more like an egg custard, with the distinct addition of clotted cream.

Ingredients

4 eggs

570 ml (1 pint) full cream milk

1 tbsp rose-water or orange flower water

$^1/_4$ tsp grated nutmeg

50 g (2 oz) caster sugar

275 ml ($^1/_2$ pint) Devon clotted cream

Large round of white bread, crusts removed and cut into slim fingers

25 g (1 oz) butter, flaked

Method

First, place the bread fingers in a large, greased ovenproof casserole. Then, in a separate basin, beat the eggs well and gradually add the milk, rosewater, nutmeg and sugar. Stir in the clotted cream and beat until combined before pouring all the mixture over the bread.

Dot with the flaked butter and bake in a moderate oven 180°C/350°F/Gas 4 for 30-35 minutes.

Devonshire cream

Mrs Beeton referred to clotted cream as 'Devonshire Cream' – clotted cream producers in Cornwall would not have been at all happy with this description. This recipe for Devonshire Cream dates back to Stuart times and uses apples and cider brandy.

Ingredients

350g (12oz) dessert apples, local if available

4 tbsp cider brandy

25g (1oz) butter

5 tbsp granulated sugar

2 eggs, beaten

275ml (1/2 pint) double cream

2 tbsp flaked almonds

Method

Cut up the peeled and cored apples and cover with the cider brandy. Allow to soak for an hour, before draining and reserving the brandy. Cook the apples over a low heat with the butter and half the sugar until soft, then divide the mixture between six small ramekins.

Mix the reserved cider brandy with the rest of the sugar, the beaten eggs and the double cream, then pour over the apples, scattering the flaked almonds over the surface.

Place the ramekins in a large baking dish, filling with hot water to a depth of about 2.5cm (1 inch), or to come half way up the ramekins. Bake in a hot oven, 200°C/400°F/Gas 6 for 20-30 minutes, until set but not too firm.

Serve either hot or cold.

Barnstaple Fair pears

The annual fair in Barnstaple takes place on the Wednesday preceding 20 September and the opening ceremony begins in the Guildhall, where a large white glove, decorated with flowers and ribbons, is suspended from the top window. The glove symbolizes an open hand of friendship, welcoming all those who trade in or visit the fair.

Pears from the local orchards always used to be sold at the fair, hence this recipe. Originally, the pears were simmered in cider but here the red wine gives a rich dark colour to the spicy, sweet fruit.

Ingredients

4 large Comice pears

25g (1oz) blanched almonds, split in half

50g (2oz) granulated sugar

275ml (1/2 pint) red wine

3 cloves

Method

Put the wine, sugar and cloves into a small pan and heat gently until the sugar has dissolved.

Remove the cores from the pears, leaving them whole, and then spike with the almond halves. Simmer the pears in the wine for 15 minutes, until they are tender but not too soft. Remove the pears and place in the serving dish.

Meanwhile, boil the liquid rapidly until reduced by half, then pour over the pears. Set aside for two hours before serving, either hot or cold, with natural yogurt or Devonshire clotted cream.

Apple and cider cakes

Many of the traditional cake recipes from Devon reflect the plentiful supply of cider in the county and, although Devon is renowned for its cider orchards, there are also many dessert and culinary varieties growing in private orchards. Devon Quarrenden, for example, was first recorded in 1678 and is a juicy, crisp apple with a strawberry taste, whereas Totnes Apple is a sweet dessert fruit and is so called because it used to be sold at Totnes Market.

Farmer's wife apple cake

This is a substantial but moist cake that can be served for afternoon tea or as a dessert, warmed with cream.

Ingredients

225g (8oz) self-raising flour

1 tsp each of mixed spice, cinnamon and ground ginger

1 tsp grated orange rind

110g (4oz) butter

110g (4oz) granulated sugar

1 egg

175g (6oz) sultanas

275g (10oz) cooking apples, peeled and chopped

1 tbsp caster sugar

Method

Sieve the flour and add the grated orange rind and spices. Cream the butter and sugar until light and fluffy, then add the egg before folding in alternate spoonfuls of flour and sultanas. Finally mix in the chopped apples.

Spoon into a base-lined 22 cm (9 inch) round cake tin and bake at 170°C/325°F/Gas 3 for 45-50 minutes, until lightly browned.

Leave to cool in the tin before turning out, sprinkle with caster sugar and serve with a jug of Devonshire double or single cream.

Apple cinnamon cake

This is another cake making use of apples, with the mixture of jam and fruit giving an interesting and colourful topping.

Ingredients

For the cake

200g (7oz) self-raising flour

85g (3oz) caster sugar

150g (5oz) soft margarine

1 egg

For the filling

2 cooking apples, peeled, cored and sliced

2 tbsp granulated sugar

2 tsp ground cinnamon

2 tbsp strawberry or blackberry jam

Method

Sieve the flour into a large bowl and add the caster sugar, soft margarine and egg.

Beat all the ingredients together with a wooden spoon until well mixed. Spoon two thirds of the mixture into a greased and lined 20cm (8 inch) round cake tin and lay the sliced apples across the mixture, then sprinkle with the granulated sugar and cinnamon.

Drop spoonfuls of the remaining mixture over the apples, without spreading, and then fill in the gaps with the jam. Take care not to place the jam too close to the edge of the cake tin, to prevent burning.

Cook for about an hour, until golden, at 180°C/350°F/Gas 4. Leave in the tin to cool before removing and placing on a wire rack.

Cider tea loaf

A tea-time loaf regularly baked in the tea rooms at Castle Drogo.

Ingredients

350g (12oz) self-raising flour

1 tsp mixed spice

110g (4oz) melted butter

110g (4oz) light brown sugar

225g (8oz) raisins

150ml (1/4 pint) milk

150ml (1/4 pint) Devon cider

1 large egg, beaten

Grated rind of one orange

Method

Sieve the flour and spices into a bowl, add the raisins, melted butter and then the brown sugar. Add the milk and cider, with the beaten egg and orange rind. Mix well with a wooden spoon until blended.

Spoon into a greased and lined 900g (2lb) loaf tin, smoothing the top before baking at 180°C/350°F/Gas 4 for 30 minutes, then reduce the oven temperature to 170°C/325°F/Gas 3 for 45 minutes, until the loaf is well risen and a skewer comes out cleanly. Turn out of the tin and cool on a wire rack.

The loaf can be eaten plain, buttered or covered with cider icing.

To ice

Mix 110g (4oz) icing sugar with 1 tsp orange juice and 1-2 tsp cider, then pour over the tea loaf.

Uffculme tea loaf

This recipe for a cider tea loaf belongs to Uffculme, near Cullompton, and it keeps well, despite the lack of butter.

Ingredients

350g (12oz) mixed dried fruit

275ml (1/2 pint) sweet cider

275g (10oz) self-raising flour

50g (2oz) chopped walnuts

175g (6oz) soft brown sugar

2 beaten eggs

Method

Grease and line a 900g (2lb) loaf tin. Soak the dried fruit in the cider overnight, then transfer to a small saucepan and bring to the boil. Leave to cool. Sieve the flour and mix in the sugar and the chopped walnuts before adding the beaten eggs, the cider and soaked fruit.

Spoon the mixture into the tin and cook at 180°C/350°F/Gas 4 for 30 minutes and then reduce the heat to 170°C/325°F/Gas 3 for about 45 minutes, or until the loaf is firm and golden brown.

Leave to cool in the tin for 5 minutes before turning out and cooling on a wire rack. Serve sliced, with or without butter.

Devonshire cider cake

A traditional cider cake, prepared more like a batter, with the mixture poured into the tin.

Ingredients

110g (4oz) butter

110g (4oz) granulated sugar

2 eggs

225g (8oz) plain flour

1/2 tsp ground ginger

1/4 tsp fresh nutmeg

1 1/2 tsp baking powder

275ml (1/2 pint) strong traditional Devon cider

Method

Cream the butter and sugar until light and fluffy and beat in the eggs before sifting in the flour, ginger, nutmeg and baking powder. Whisk the cider until frothy, then beat it into the cake batter.

Pour into a lined round 20cm (8 inch) cake tin and bake for 45 minutes – 1 hour at 180°C/350°F/Gas 4, until golden.

Other cakes, scones and biscuits

Dripping cake

An old-fashioned farmhouse fruit cake, making use of the dripping from the Sunday roast. Pork dripping is best but, if that is unavailable, lard can be substituted.

Ingredients

450g (1lb) plain flour	175g (6oz) dripping or lard
50g (2oz) candied peel	225g (8oz) raisins or sultanas
175g (6oz) light brown sugar	1 generous tbsp black treacle
2 eggs	1 tsp bicarbonate of soda
Approximately 275ml (1/2 pint) milk	

Method

Sift the flour into a bowl and rub in the dripping or lard until the mixture resembles coarse breadcrumbs. Add the peel and raisins, followed by the sugar. Fold in the well-beaten eggs, the treacle and most of the milk. Warm the remaining milk and add the bicarbonate of soda. Mix this into the cake mixture, which should then drop easily from the spoon.

Turn into a greased and lined 25cm (10 inch) round cake tin and bake at 180°C/350°F/Gas 4 for 1 1/2 hours, lowering the temperature towards the end of the cooking time to prevent over browning. Leave to cool before removing from the tin. The cake keeps well and is best stored in an air-tight tin.

Old folk's tea cake

This substantial family cake with a good almond flavour was served by Glenorchy United Reformed Church, Exmouth, at an annual event from the 1890s to around 1975.

Ingredients

350g (12oz) self-raising flour	225g (8oz) margarine
225g (8oz)soft brown sugar	225g (8oz) raisins
110g (4oz) ground almonds	1/2 tsp almond essence
3 eggs	100ml (1/2 cup) of cold water

Method

Cream the margarine before adding the sugar, beating well. Add eggs with a little of the flour before mixing in the rest of the flour. Add the almonds, essence and raisins, then the water last of all, making a moist mixture. Spoon into a greased and lined round 20 cm (8 inch) tin and bake for approximately 1 1/4 hours, at 180°C/350°F/Gas 4, lowering the temperature to 170°C/325°F/Gas 3 towards the end of the cooking time.

Exeter sandwich

This recipe is said to be 200 years old. Exeter sandwich is a cross between a pudding and a sponge cake and the method is unusual: the mixture is rolled out like pastry to fit the tin, with the two layers sandwiched together with raspberry jam before baking.

Ingredients

225 g (8 oz) plain flour (although self-raising flour is equally successful and results in a deeper 'sandwich')

110 g (4 oz) caster sugar

110 g (4 oz) butter

1 beaten egg

3-4 tbsp raspberry jam

50 g (2 oz) flaked almonds

Method

Rub the butter into the flour, add the sugar and mix in the beaten egg. Knead lightly and then halve the mixture. Roll out one half to fit into a greased and base-lined 18 cm (7 inch) sandwich tin, press into the tin and cover generously with raspberry jam. Cover this with the second round, pressing the edges firmly to seal in the jam. Scatter the almonds over the surface.

Bake for 40 minutes at 180°C/350°F/Gas 4. Traditionally, Exeter sandwich is served cold, with a large scoop of Devonshire clotted cream, but some people prefer it warm from the oven.

Honey cake

Dark Exmoor heather honey is ideal for this rich, golden honey cake although other types of honey can be used. Honey is now regarded as a luxury food but it was more plentiful in the past and was the usual ingredient for sweetening.

Ingredients

175 g (6 oz) Exmoor heather honey

150 g (5 oz) butter

85 g (3 oz) soft brown sugar

1 egg

200 g (7 oz) self-raising flour

1 tsp baking powder

1 tbsp water

For the glaze

1 tbsp honey

1 tbsp water

2 tbsp sieved icing sugar

Method

Put the honey, sugar, butter and water in a small pan and heat gently, without allowing the mixture to boil. Add the beaten egg, then the sieved flour and baking powder and mix together. Spoon into a lined round 20 cm (8 inch) cake tin and bake at 180°C/350°F/Gas 4 for 45 minutes, covering the cake with foil for the last 10 minutes to prevent over-browning. Leave to cool in the tin.

Warm the ingredients for the glaze – the honey, water and icing sugar – and brush over the surface of the cake. Turn out when cold.

Cream teas

Sampling a cream tea is now an essential ingredient for a holiday in Devon. Whether scones or splits are chosen, they have to be eaten in the Devon way, spread generously with thick Devonshire clotted cream and topped with local strawberry jam. At one time, jam was more expensive than the cream and was used sparingly, but now strawberries are plentiful. In Combe Martin, in North Devon, there is even an annual Strawberry Fayre in June, celebrating the local harvest. Clotted cream always used to be made in the farm kitchen, but nowadays commercially made cream is readily obtainable.

Cream teas are said to have originated in Tavistock in the eleventh century, when the Benedictine monks at Tavistock Abbey rewarded the workmen who were re-building the monastery with home made bread, covered with jam and clotted cream. Later and more traditionally, splits or cut rounds or chudleighs, as they are called in some parts of Devon, became the norm, but now they have generally been replaced by scones.

Honey scones

What better way to enjoy a cream tea than with honey scones made with rich Exmoor honey? A hint of lavender from North Devon can be added as an optional extra.

Ingredients

450g (1lb) plain flour   1 tsp bicarbonate of soda

2 tsp cream of tartar   275ml ($^1/_2$ pint) of milk

1 tbsp of Exmoor or other local honey, warmed

1 tsp sieved English lavender powder (optional)

Method

Sift the dry ingredients together, warm the honey until lukewarm and add to the milk. Mix the milk and honey into the dry ingredients, knead lightly and roll out on a floured board to a thickness of about 2cm ($^3/_4$ inch).

Cut into rounds, using a 6cm (2$^1/_2$ inch) cutter and place on greased baking trays. Bake at 200°C/400°F/Gas 6 for 8 minutes.

Widecombe Fair gingerbreads

Widecombe Fair was first held as a livestock fair on 29 October 1850, when cattle, sheep and Dartmoor ponies were sold on Widecombe Green, and it became an annual event. In the 1920s a sports day for local children was introduced and arts and craft stalls made their appearance in the 1930s.

Nowadays it is held in the Fair Field on the second Tuesday in September, with Uncle Tom Cobley putting in an attendance in fancy dress.

Gingerbreads or fairings used to be sold at the country fairs throughout Devon. The following is a traditional recipe for Widecombe gingerbreads.

Ingredients

85g (3oz) soft brown sugar

60g (2¹/₂oz) butter

85g (3oz) black treacle

175g (6oz) plain flour

1 tsp ground ginger

1 tbsp milk

Pinch of bicarbonate of soda

Pinch of salt

Method

Cream the sugar and butter until soft, add the black treacle and mix well before adding the flour and ginger. Warm the milk and add the bicarbonate of soda, then add to the dry ingredients with a pinch of salt.

Once mixed into a pliable dough, roll into walnut sized balls and place on a well greased baking tray. Bake at 190°C/375°F/Gas 5 for 10-15 minutes.

Preserves

Rhubarb jam

Rhubarb jam often has a bitter taste and low keeping quality but this recipe from a Victorian hand-written collection keeps well, retaining both flavour and colour.

Ingredients

  1.35 kg (3 lb) fresh rhubarb, washed, trimmed and sliced

  1.35 kg (3 lb) preserving sugar

  1 lemon, rind and juice

  1 tsp almond essence

  1 tsp ground cinnamon

  1 tsp ground ginger

  A handful of fresh blackberries, to give colour (optional)

Method

Wash the rhubarb and chop into 2.5 cm (1 inch) slices. Place into a large preserving pan with the lemon rind, spices and almond essence. A few blackberries can be added at this stage to give the jam a deeper colour.

Simmer over a gentle heat for about 1 1/2 hours, until the rhubarb is reduced to a pulp. Only add water if the rhubarb is in danger of burning. Add the preserving sugar with the lemon juice, then boil rapidly until setting point is reached. This can be judged by putting a spoonful of the hot jam on a cold saucer. If the jam ripples when pushed with a finger, it is ready to pour into sterilised, heated jars. Cover and label.

Dittisham plum jam

Dittisham plums are unique. They only grow in Dittisham, in the Dart Valley of South Devon, and as they have a short season, they are much sought after when they are available, towards the end of July and beginning of August. Similar to a Victoria Plum and dark red in colour, the Plowman Plum, as it is known locally, is thought to have been introduced into Devon from Germany.

Plum jam is always satisfying to make because it sets well and has good keeping qualities. The only disadvantage is having to remove the stones!

Ingredients

1.35 kg (3 lb) Dittisham plums (or similar variety), washed and stones removed

1.35 kg (3 lb) preserving sugar

275 ml (1/2 pint) water

Method

Wash the plums and remove the stones. (If preferred, the stones can be removed as the fruit is boiling, when they rise to the surface, or they can be sieved out of the jam before the sugar is added.)

Put the plums into a preserving pan, with the water, and simmer until the fruit is tender. Add the sugar, stirring until dissolved and then boil rapidly until setting point is reached. This can be determined by putting a spoonful of jam on a cold saucer and pushing forward with a finger. If it wrinkles, setting point has been reached. Remove any scum from the jam, pour into heated, sterilised jars, seal and label.